Your first 100 words in

JAPANESE

Beginner's Quick & Easy Guide to Demystifying Japanese Script

Series concept
Jane Wightwick

Illustrations
Mahmoud Gaafar

Japanese edition
Kazumi Honda

PASSPORT BOOKS
NTC/Contemporary Publishing Group

Other titles in this series:

Your First 100 Words in Arabic
Your First 100 Words in Chinese
Your First 100 Words in Russian

Cover design by Nick Panos

Published by Passport Books
A division of NTC/Contemporary Publishing Group, Inc.
4255 West Touhy Avenue, Lincolnwood (Chicago), Illinois 60712-1975 U.S.A.
Copyright © 1999 by Gaafar & Wightwick
Printed in the United States of America
International Standard Book Number: 0-8442-2396-4

2 3 4 5 6 7 8 9   VLP/VLP   0 5 4 3 2 1

◎ CONTENTS

◎ INTRODUCTION

In this activity book you'll find 100 key words for you to learn to read in Japanese. All of the activities are designed specifically for reading non-Latin script languages. Many of the activities are inspired by the kind of games used to teach children to read their own language: flashcards, matching games, memory games, joining exercises, etc. This is not only a more effective method of learning to read a new script, but also much more fun.

We've included a **Scriptbreaker** to get you started. This is a friendly introduction to the Japanese script that will give you tips on how to remember the characters.

Then you can move on to the eight **Topics**. Each topic presents essential words in large type. There is also a pronunciation guide so you know how to say the words. These words are also featured in the tear-out **Flashcard** section at the back of the book. When you've mastered the words, you can go on to try out the activities and games for that topic.

There's also a **Round-up** section to review all your new words and the **Answers** to all the activities to check yourself.

Follow this 4-step plan for maximum success:

1 Have a look at the key topic words with their pictures. Then tear out the flashcards and shuffle them. Put them Japanese side up. Try to remember what the word means and turn the card over to check with the English. When you can do this, cover the pronunciation and try to say the word and remember the meaning by looking at the Japanese script only.

2 Put the cards English side up and try to say the Japanese word. Try the cards again each day both ways around. (When you can remember a card for seven days in a row, you can file it.)

3 Try out the activities and games for each topic. This will reinforce your recognition of the key words.

4 After you have covered all the topics, you can try the activities in the **Round-up** section to test your knowledge of all the 100 words in the book. You can also try shuffling all the flashcards together to see how many you can remember.

This flexible and fun way of reading your first words in Japanese should give you a head start whether you're learning at home or in a group.

◎ SCRIPTBREAKER

The purpose of this Scriptbreaker is to introduce you to the Japanese script and how it is formed. You should not try to memorize the characters at this stage, nor try to write the words yourself. Instead, have a quick look through this section and then move on to the topics, glancing back if you want to work out the characters in a particular word. Remember, though, that recognizing the whole shape of the word in an unfamiliar script is just as important as knowing how it is made up. Using this method you will have a much more instinctive recall of vocabulary and will gain the confidence to expand your knowledge in other directions.

No-one can pretend that the Japanese writing system is simple. For historic reasons, the Japanese language is written in a combination of three different scripts: *kanji*, the Chinese system of ideograms adopted by Japanese; *hiragana*, a script used mainly for words of Japanese origin; and *katakana*, a script used to write foreign loan words, of which there are many.

Although it is possible to write all words in *katakana*, and indeed this is how Japanese children first learn to write, there is a commonly-accepted way of writing a particular word and this is the one you would see in everyday life. The aim of this book is for you to recognize the word as it is normally written.

◎ Kanji

Kanji is not an alphabet, but a series of ideograms, or "characters." These characters originally evolved in China out of pictograms used as a writing system by primitive hunters and were then adopted by Japanese. A few characters still resemble the object or concept they refer to, but most have changed beyond recognition.

Japanese uses *kanji* to write basic words and concepts. So you will find that, for example, most words connected with the natural world or universal concepts, such as "big" and "small," will be represented by *kanji*, or a combination of *kanji* with added *hiragana*.

Some words consist of a single *kanji*:

mountain 山 (*yama*)

car 車 (*kuruma*)

sheep 羊 (*hitsuji*)

Other words are made up of two or more *kanji*:

train 列車 (*ressha*)

farm 畑 (*nohara*)

There is no way of working out the pronunciation of *kanji*, you have to learn them on an individual basis.

- ✔ *Kanji* is the system of Chinese ideograms which are used to write many basic Japanese words
- ✔ *Kanji* have to be learnt on an individual basis

◎ Katakana

Although often referred to as an "alphabet," *katakana* is actually a "syllabary." Each character represents a syllable (a consonant plus a vowel), such as *"ha"* or *"fu."*

In addition, the signs ﹅ and ° are used to add further sounds. A long dash (一) will lengthen a sound. For example, the *katakana* character テ (*"te"*) is lengthened to テー (*"tee"*) by adding this dash:

table テーブル (*teeburu*)

sweater セーター (*seetaa*)

Below is the full *katakana* syllabary, but do not try to learn it off by heart. It is better to give these tables a quick glance and then move on to the topics. As you meet each word, you can refer to this Scriptbreaker if you want to work out the individual characters that make up the word.

ア a	カ ka	サ sa	タ ta	ナ na	ハ ha	マ ma	ヤ ya	ラ ra	ワ wa
イ i	キ ki	シ shi	チ chi	ニ ni	ヒ hi	ミ mi		リ ri	
ウ u	ク ku	ス su	ツ tsu	ヌ nu	フ fu	ム mu	ユ yu	ル ru	
エ e	ケ ke	セ se	テ te	ネ ne	ヘ he	メ me		レ re	
オ o	コ ko	ソ so	ト to	ノ no	ホ ho	モ mo	ヨ yo	ロ ro	ヲ (w)o
				ン n					

◎ Hiragana

Like *katakana*, *hiragana* is a syllabary. The signs ˝ and º can also be added to a hiragana character to add further sounds.

Some words are written entirely in *hiragana*:

clean　きれい　(*kirii*)

Many others are made up of a *kanji* ideogram with a *hirgana* ending:

big　大きい　(*ookii*)

new　新しい　(*atarashii*)

Here is the complete *hiragana* syllabary:

あ a	か ka	さ sa	た ta	な na	は ha	ま ma	や ya	ら ra	わ wa
い i	き ki	し shi	ち chi	に ni	ひ hi	み mi		り ri	
う u	く ku	す su	つ tsu	ぬ nu	ふ fu	む mu	ゆ yu	る ru	
え e	け ke	せ se	て te	ね ne	へ he	め me		れ re	
お o	こ ko	そ so	と to	の no	ほ ho	も mo	よ yo	ろ ro	を (w)o
				ん n					

* ✔ *Hiragana* and *katakana* are the syllabary scripts used to write Japanese in addition to *kanji*
* ✔ *Katakana* is used to write words of foreign origin
* ✔ *Hiragana* is also used to add endings to *kanji*

Pronuncation tips

The syllables in Japanese are pronounced equally and there is no particular emphasis on any part of the word. Many letters are pronounced in a similar way to English, but look out for these more unfamiliar sounds:

f   a Japanese "f" is pronounced without putting your lower teeth over your upper lip

r   somewhere between the English "r"and "l"

w   pronounced with slack rather than rounded lips

✔ Many Japanese letters are pronounced in a similar way to English

✔ Generally, Japanese does not emphasize a particular part of a word or pronounce letters with rounded lips or teeth against lips.

① AROUND THE HOME

Look at the pictures of things you might find in a house.
Tear out the flashcards for this topic.
Follow steps 1 and 2 of the plan in the introduction.

テーブル
teeburu

テレビ
terebi

窓
mado

椅子
isu

コンピュータ
konpyuutaa

電話
denwa

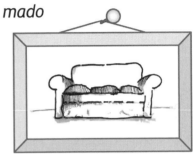

ソフア *sofaa*

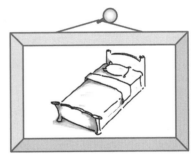

ベッド *beddo*

冷蔵庫
reezooko

戸棚
todana

レンジ
renji

ドア
doa

◎ **M**atch the pictures with the words, as in the example.

ソファ

ベッド

窓

テーブル

テレビ

コンピュータ

電話

椅子

◎ **N**ow match the Japanese household words to the English.

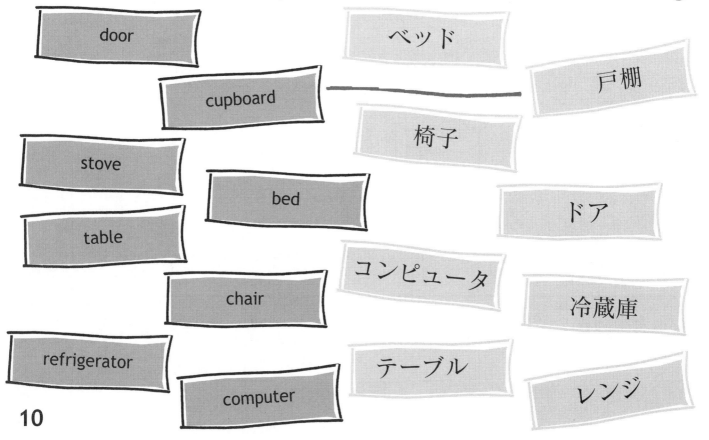

door

cupboard

stove

bed

table

chair

refrigerator

computer

ベッド

戸棚

椅子

ドア

コンピュータ

冷蔵庫

テーブル

レンジ

◎ Match the words and their pronunciation.

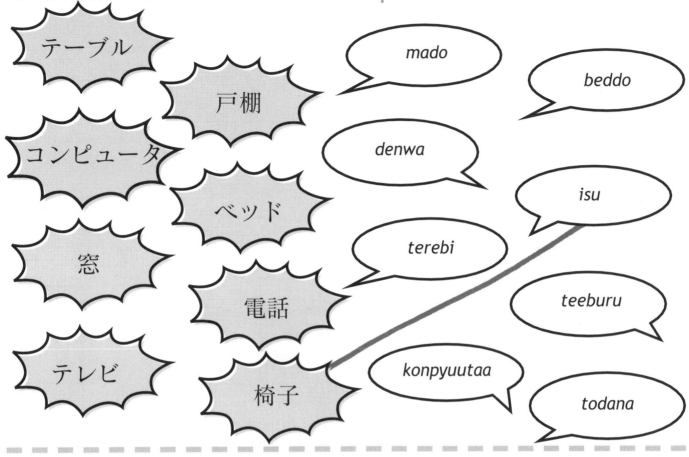

- -

◎ See if you can find these words in the word square.
The words can run left to right, or top to bottom:

レンジ

ベッド

椅子

冷蔵庫

ドア

ソファ

背	自	い	バ	い	ル	中	ス
車	椅	子	橋	子	安	館	き
コ	い	ン	ソ	コ	ベ	ユ	き
牛	一	安	フ	画	ッ	ン	ド
ン	ピ	ス	ァ	殻	ド	高	ア
い	い	花	さ	い	重	い	ん
レ	ン	ジ	こ	ち	は	な	い
は	こ	重	丘	冷	蔵	庫	軽

11

Decide where the household items should go. Then write the correct number in the picture, as in the example.

1. テーブル   2. 椅子   3. ソファ   4. テレビ
5. 電話   6. ベッド   7. 戸棚   8. レンジ
9. 冷蔵庫   10. コンピュータ   11. 窓   12. ドア

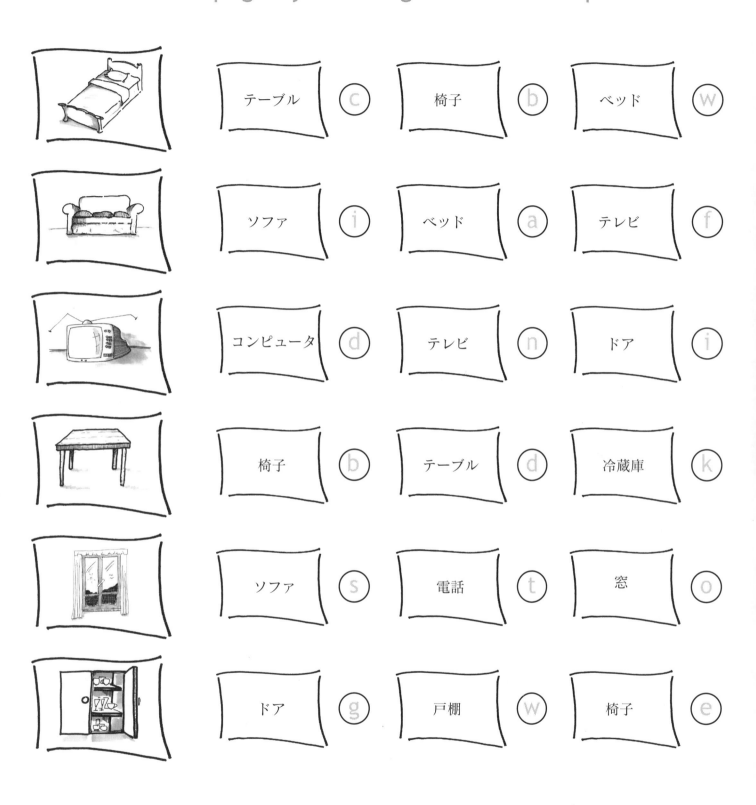

○ **N**ow see if you can fill in the household word at the bottom of the page by choosing the correct Japanese.

テーブル (c)	椅子 (b)	ベッド (w)
ソファ (i)	ベッド (a)	テレビ (f)
コンピュータ (d)	テレビ (n)	ドア (i)
椅子 (b)	テーブル (d)	冷蔵庫 (k)
ソファ (s)	電話 (t)	窓 (o)
ドア (g)	戸棚 (w)	椅子 (e)

English word: (w) ( ) ( ) ( ) ( ) ( )

② CLOTHES

Look at the pictures of different clothes.
Tear out the flashcards for this topic.
Follow steps 1 and 2 of the plan in the introduction.

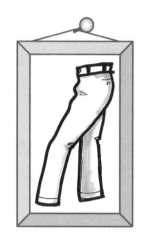

ベルト
beruto

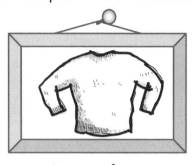

セーター
seetaa

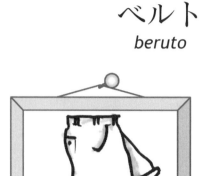

半ズボン
hanzubon

ズボン
zubon

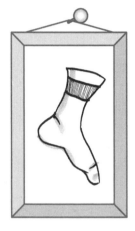

ソックス
sokk(u)su

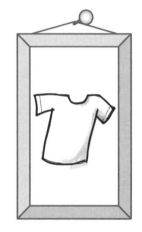

Ｔシャツ
tiishatsu

コート
kooto

スカート
s(u)kaato

ワンピース
wanpiisu

帽子　*booshi*

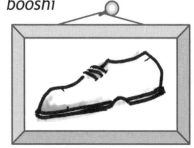

靴　*kutsu*

ワイシャツ　*waishatsu*

◎ **M**atch the Japanese words and their pronunciation.

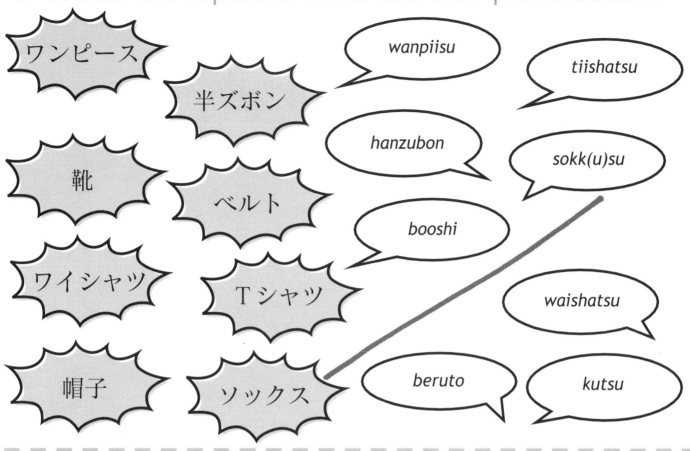

ワンピース

半ズボン

靴

ベルト

ワイシャツ

Tシャツ

帽子

ソックス

wanpiisu

tiishatsu

hanzubon

sokk(u)su

booshi

waishatsu

beruto

kutsu

◎ **S**ee if you can find these clothes in the word square.

The words can run left to right, or top to bottom:

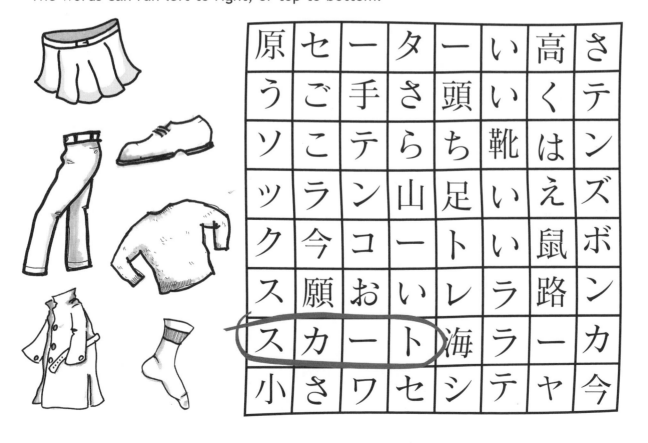

原	セ	ー	タ	ー	い	高	さ
う	ご	手	さ	頭	い	く	テ
ソ	こ	テ	ら	ち	靴	は	ン
ッ	ラ	ン	山	足	い	え	ズ
ク	今	コ	ー	ト	い	鼠	ボ
ス	願	お	い	レ	ラ	路	ン
ス	カ	ー	ト	海	ラ	ー	カ
小	さ	ワ	セ	シ	テ	ャ	今

Now match the Japanese words, their pronunciation, and the English meaning, as in the example.

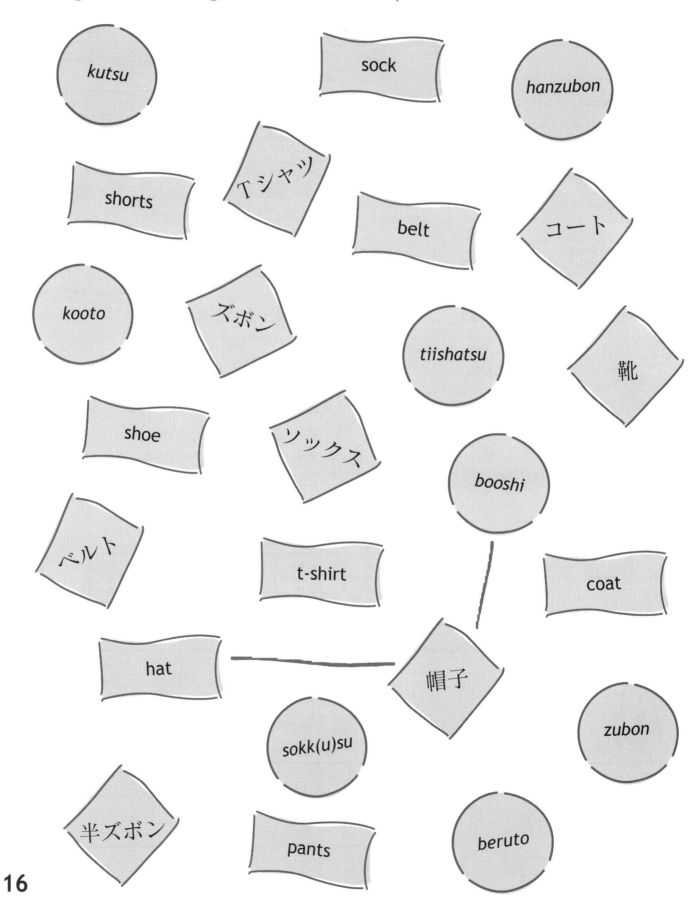

kutsu

sock

hanzubon

shorts

Tシャツ

belt

コート

kooto

ズボン

tiishatsu

靴

shoe

ソックス

booshi

ベルト

t-shirt

coat

hat

帽子

zubon

sokk(u)su

半ズボン

pants

beruto

◎ Candy is going on vacation. Count how many of each type of clothing she is packing in her suitcase.

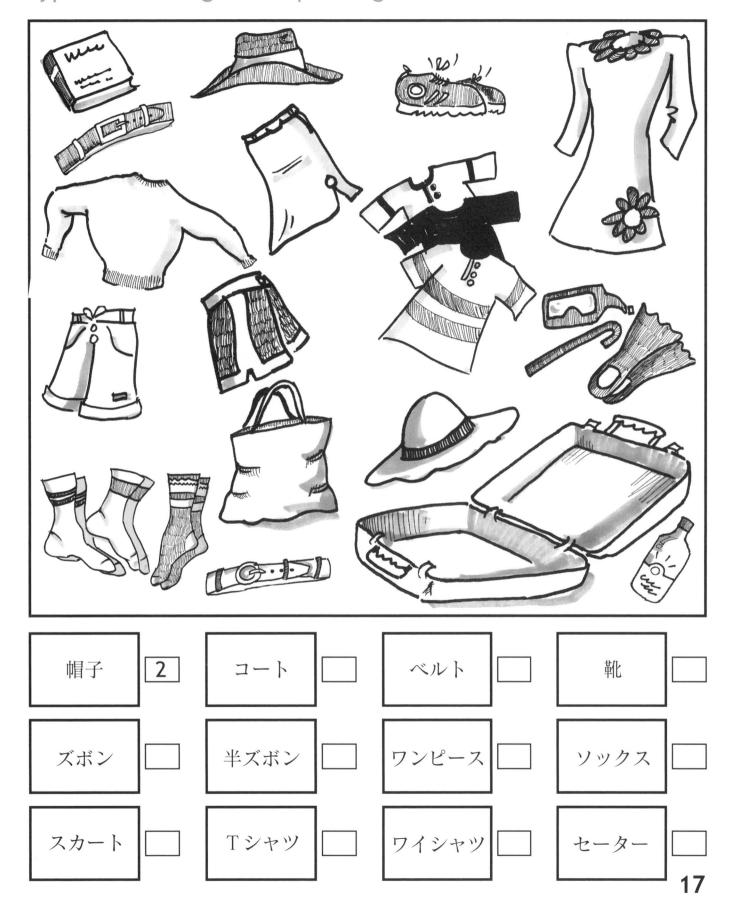

帽子	2	コート		ベルト		靴	
ズボン		半ズボン		ワンピース		ソックス	
スカート		Ｔシャツ		ワイシャツ		セーター	

Someone has ripped up the Japanese words for clothes.
Can you join the two halves of the words, as the example?

❸ AROUND TOWN

Look at the pictures of things you might around town.
Tear out the flashcards for this topic.
Follow steps 1 and 2 of the plan in the introduction.

ホテル *hoteru*

バス
basu

家
ie

車
kuruma

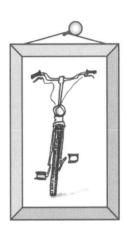
自転車
jitensha

映画館
eegakan

列車
ressha

タクシー *tak(u)shii*

学校 *gakkoo*

道路 *dooro*

店 *mise*

レストラン
res(u)toran

◎ **M**atch the Japanese words to their English equivalents.

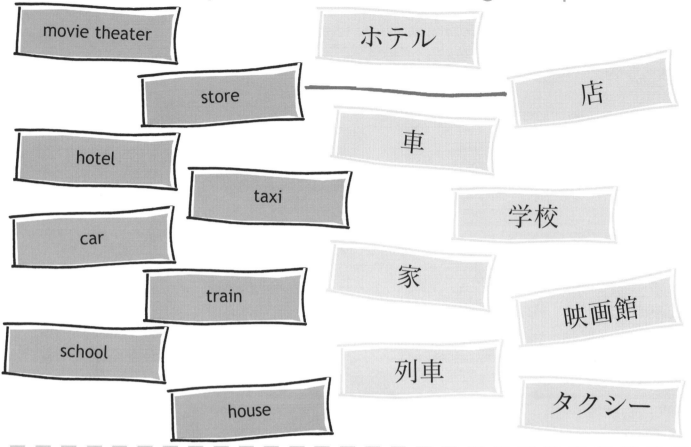

movie theater

store

ホテル

店

車

hotel

taxi

学校

car

家

train

映画館

school

列車

house

タクシー

- -

◎ **N**ow list the correct order of the English words to match the Japanese word chain, as in the example.

バス — 家 — 道路 — 自転車 — 車 — 列車 — タクシー

bicycle   taxi   house   bus   train   road   car

4 ___ ___ ___ ___ ___ ___

◎ Match the words to the signs.

学校　　　　　　車　　　　自転車　　　　バス

レストラン　　　列車　　　　ホテル　　　　タクシー

Now choose the Japanese word that matches the picture to fill in the English word at the bottom of the page.

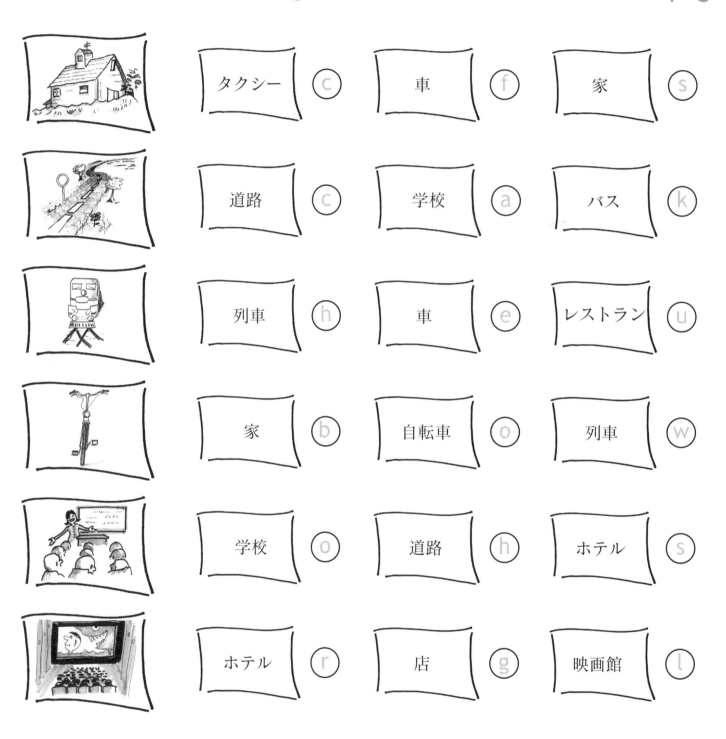

English word: (s) ( ) ( ) ( ) ( ) ( )

Now match the Japanese to the pronunciation.

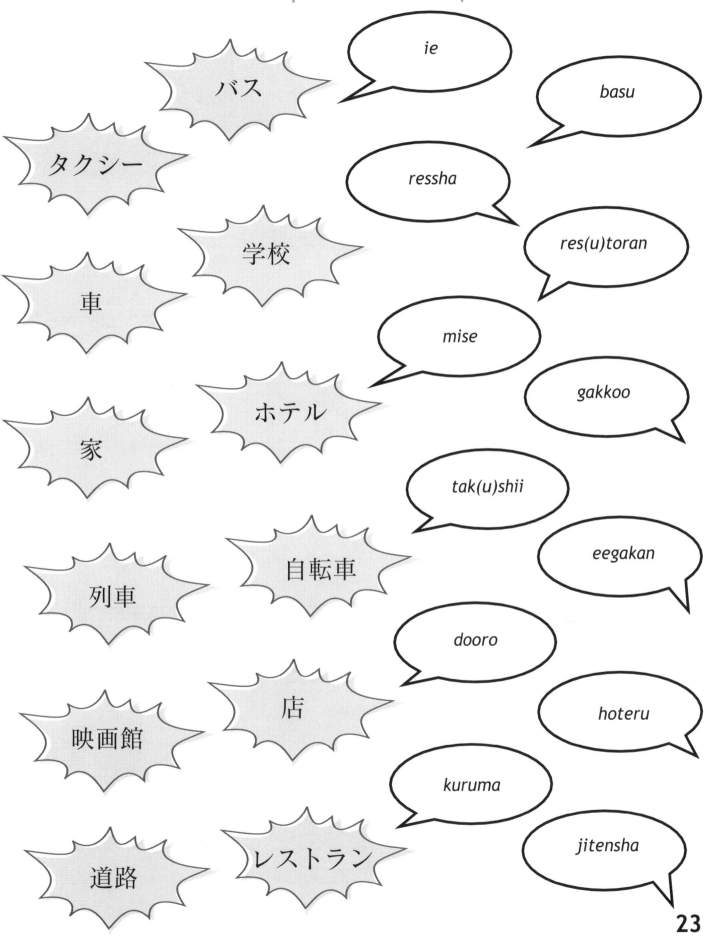

❹ COUNTRYSIDE

Look at the pictures of things you might find in the countryside.
Tear out the flashcards for this topic.
Follow steps 1 and 2 of the plan in the introduction.

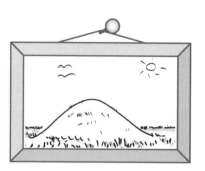

丘 *oka*

橋
hashi

畑
hatake

山 *yama*

湖
mizu'umi

木 *ki*

花
hana

川 *kawa*

海 *umi*

野原 *nohara*

砂漠 *sabaku*

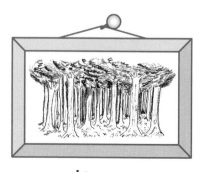

森 *mori*

🌀 **C**an you match all the countryside words to the pictures.

山
畑
海
森
砂漠
丘
湖
橋
川
花
木
野原

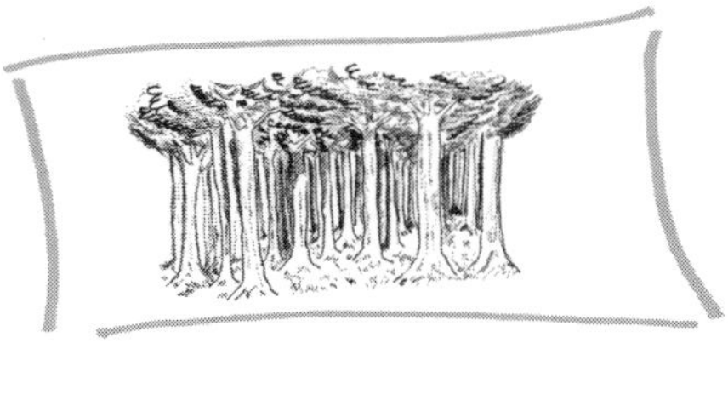

25

◎ **N**ow check (✔) the features you can find in this landscape.

橋 ✔   木 ☐   砂漠 ☐   丘 ☐

山 ☐   海 ☐   野原 ☐   森 ☐

湖 ☐   川 ☐   花 ☐   畑 ☐

◎ **M**atch the Japanese words and their pronunciation.

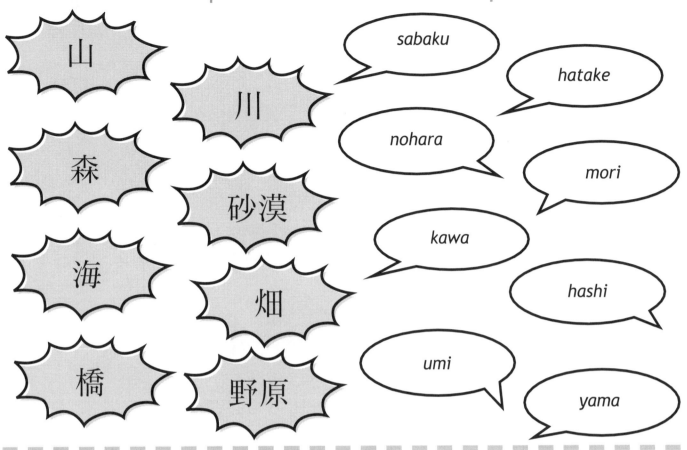

- -

◎ **S**ee if you can find these words in the word square.
The words can run left to right, or top to bottom.

木
畑
丘
花
橋
湖

湖	ベ	き	車	き	ド	中	コ
ト	タ	ン	ピ	映	ト	丘	ン
ス	汚	畑	棚	ス	い	い	耳
速	い	す	よ	な	い	に	帽
子	い	イ	足	花	く	鼠	ン
お	兎	い	新	い	口	路	校
木	蔵	兎	ラ	ン	ー	橋	ス
ト	店	ボ	羊	ツ	み	す	ん

◎ **F**inally, test yourself by joining the Japanese words, their pronunciation, and the English meanings, as in the example.

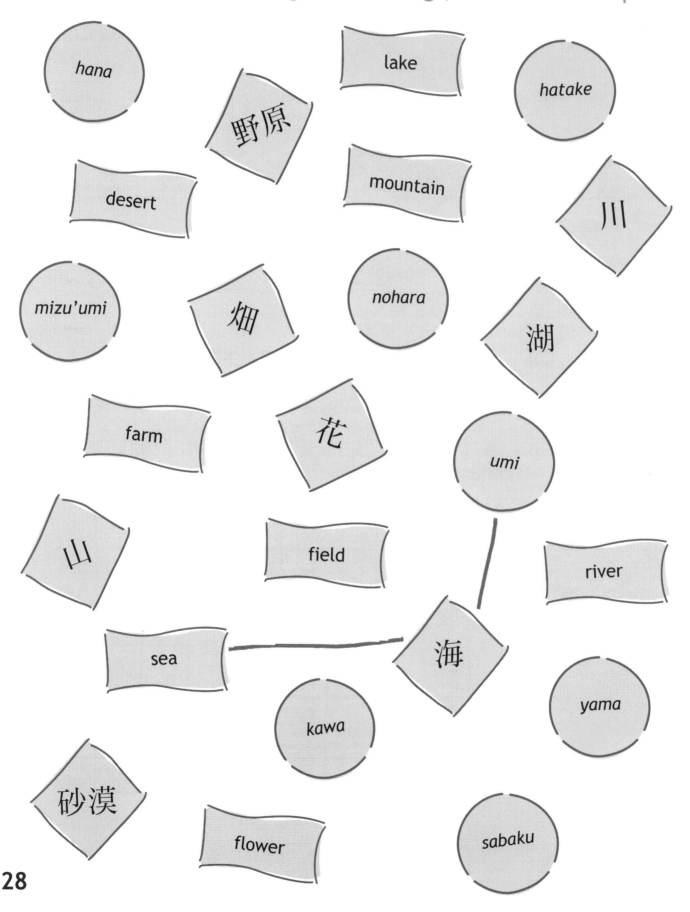

hana

lake

hatake

野原

mountain

desert

川

mizu'umi

畑

nohara

湖

farm

花

umi

山

field

river

sea

海

kawa

yama

砂漠

flower

sabaku

❺ OPPOSITES

Look at the pictures.
Tear out the flashcards for this topic.
Follow steps 1 and 2 of the plan in the introduction.

汚い
kitanai

きれい
kiree

小さい
chiisai

大きい
ookii

安い
yasui

軽い *karui*

遅い *osoi*

高い *takai*

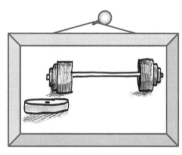

重い *omoi*

速い *hayai*

古い *furui*

新しい *atarashii*

Join the Japanese words to their English equivalents.

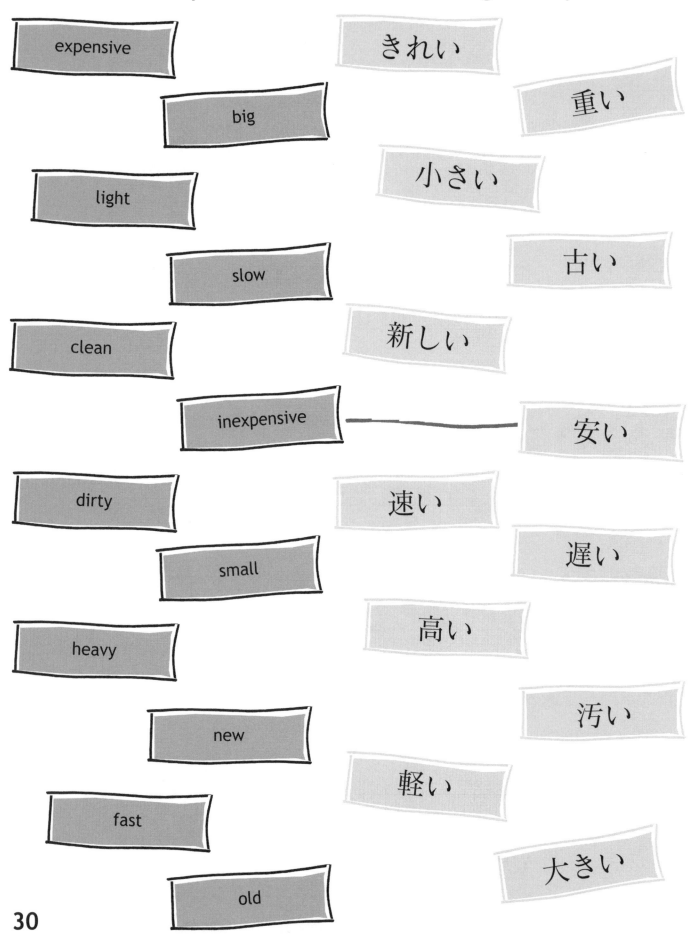

expensive

きれい

重い

big

小さい

light

古い

slow

新しい

clean

inexpensive ———————— 安い

速い

dirty

遅い

small

高い

heavy

汚い

new

軽い

fast

大きい

old

◎ **N**ow choose the Japanese word that matches the
picture to fill in the English word at the bottom of the page.

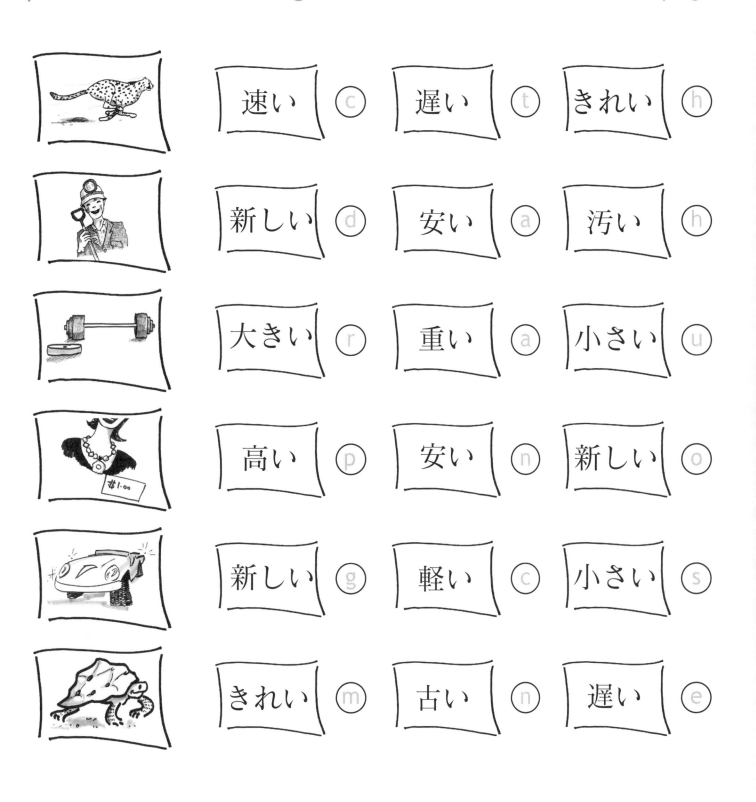

速い	ⓒ	遅い	ⓣ	きれい	ⓗ
新しい	ⓓ	安い	ⓐ	汚い	ⓗ
大きい	ⓡ	重い	ⓐ	小さい	ⓤ
高い	ⓟ	安い	ⓝ	新しい	ⓞ
新しい	ⓖ	軽い	ⓒ	小さい	ⓢ
きれい	ⓜ	古い	ⓝ	遅い	ⓔ

English word: ○ ○ ○ ○ ○ ○

Find the odd one out in these groups of words.

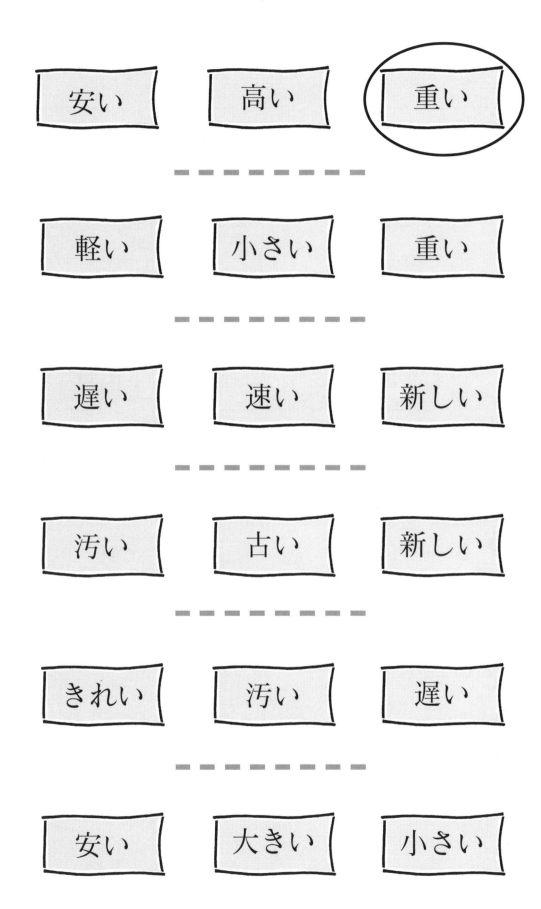

安い　高い　重い

軽い　小さい　重い

遅い　速い　新しい

汚い　古い　新しい

きれい　汚い　遅い

安い　大きい　小さい

◎ **F**inally, join the English words to their Japanese opposites, as in the example.

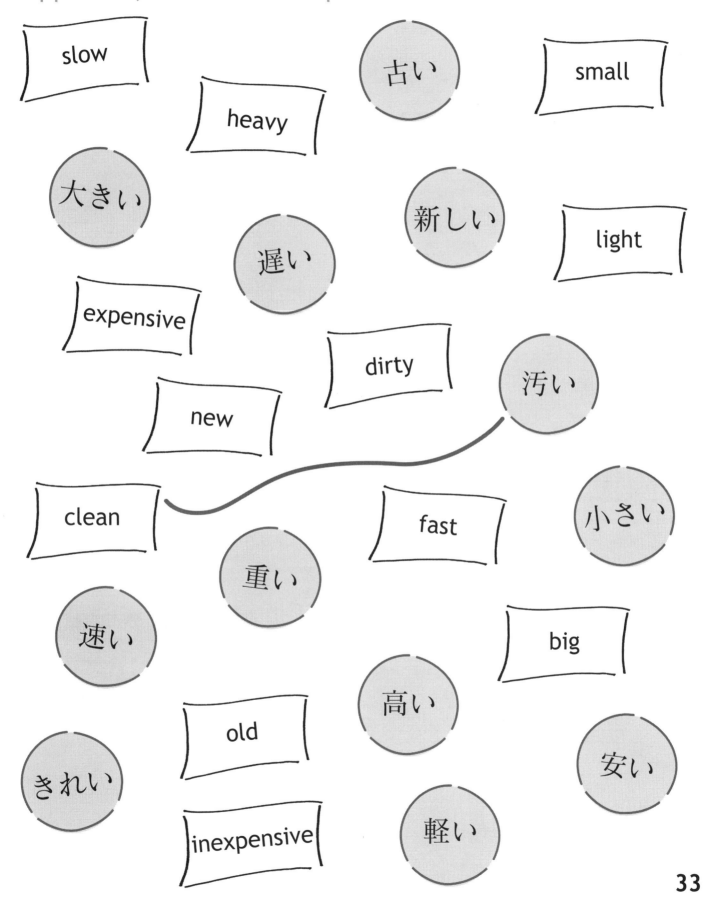

slow

heavy

古い

small

大きい

新しい

light

遅い

expensive

dirty

汚い

new

clean

fast

小さい

重い

速い

big

きれい

old

高い

安い

inexpensive

軽い

❻ ANIMALS

Look at the pictures.
Tear out the flashcards for this topic.
Follow steps 1 and 2 of the plan in the introduction.

鴨 *kamo*

象 *zoo*

猫 *neko*

犬 *inu*

兎 *usagi*

猿 *saru*

魚 *sakana*

羊 *hitsuji*

鼠 *nezumi*

牛 *ushi*

馬 *uma*

ライオン *raion*

 **M**atch the animals to their associated pictures, as in the example.

兎

馬

猿

猫

羊

鼠

犬

牛　ライオン

魚

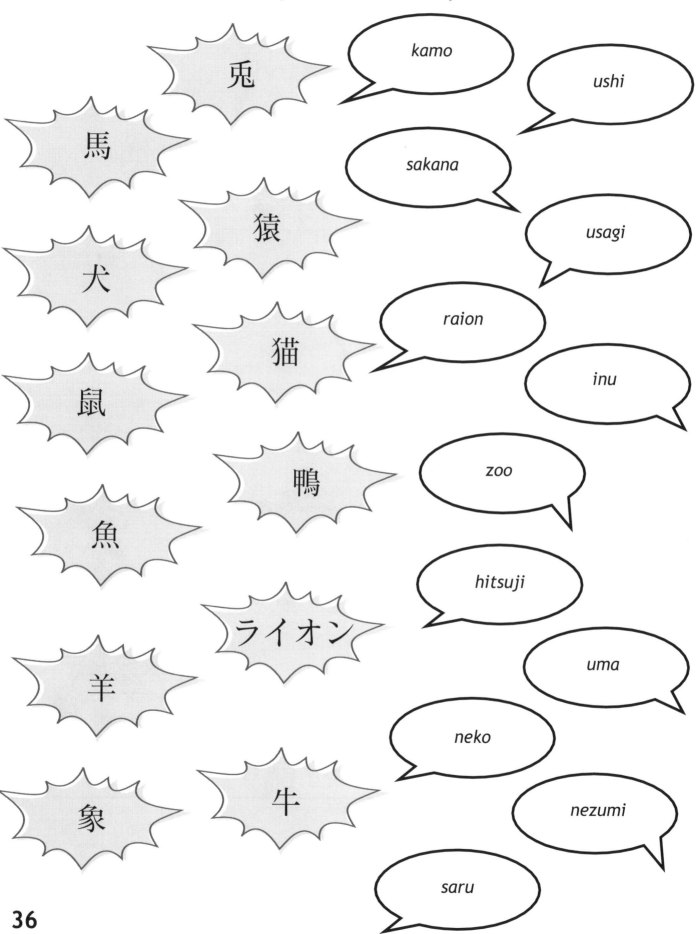

Check (✔) the animal words you can find in the word pile.

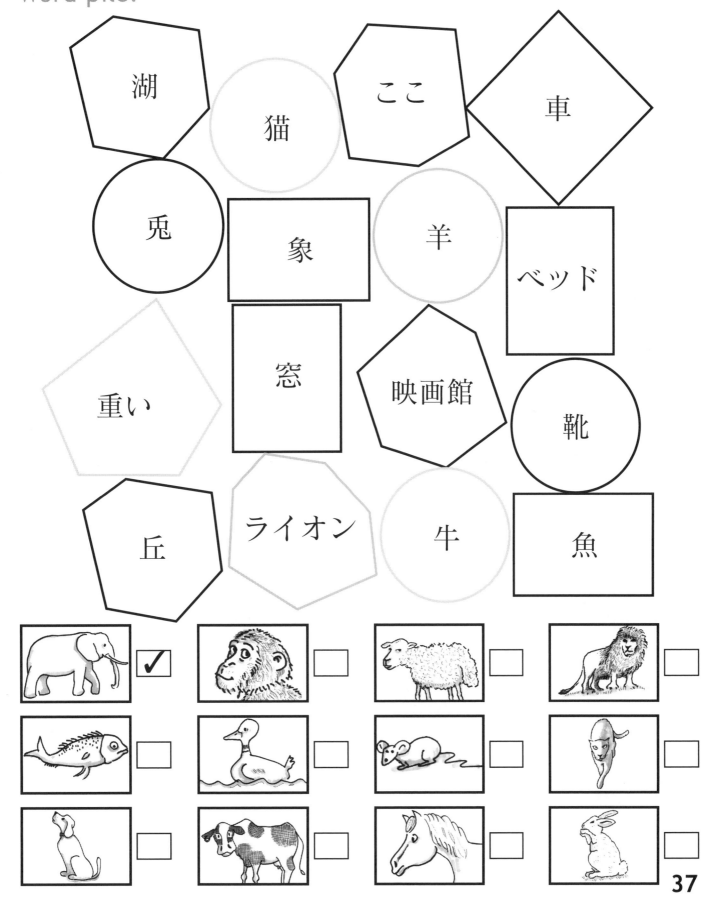

湖

猫

ここ

車

兎

象

羊

ベッド

重い

窓

映画館

靴

丘

ライオン

牛

魚

Join the Japanese animals to their English equivalents.

monkey

犬

ライオン

cow

猿

mouse

象

dog

兎

sheep

fish ———— 魚

lion

鼠

elephant

鴨

cat

牛

duck

羊

rabbit

馬

horse

猫

7 PARTS OF THE BODY

Look at the pictures of parts of the body.
Tear out the flashcards for this topic.
Follow steps 1 and 2 of the plan in the introduction.

指 *yubi*

頭 *atama*

腕 *ude*

目 *me*

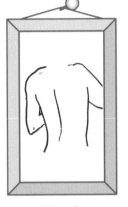

背中 *senaka*

手 *te*

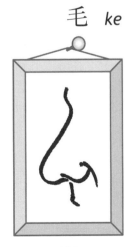

毛 *ke*

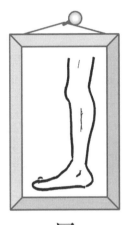

足 *ashi*

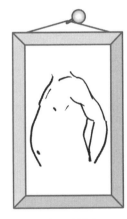

お腹 *onaka*

耳 *mimi*

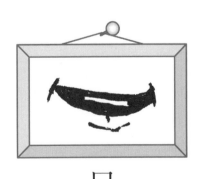

鼻 *hana*

口 *kuchi*

39

Someone has ripped up the Japanese words for parts of the body. Can you join the two halves of the word again?

ツ	ド	ス	安	い	子	大	い
鼻	映	館	口	き	ピ	毛	一
犬	ス	汚	象	森	よ	ら	さ
ご	い	に	は	こ	ル	テ	家
く	ら	今	古	い	耳	鼠	ラ
ン	軽	川	ラ	兎	靴	お	ラ
ん	足	ジ	ー	シ	ソ	ス	あ
日	ズ	木	ン	目	昨	は	こ

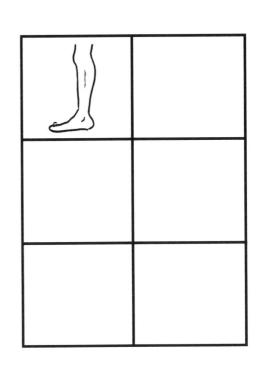

Now match the Japanese to the pronunciation.

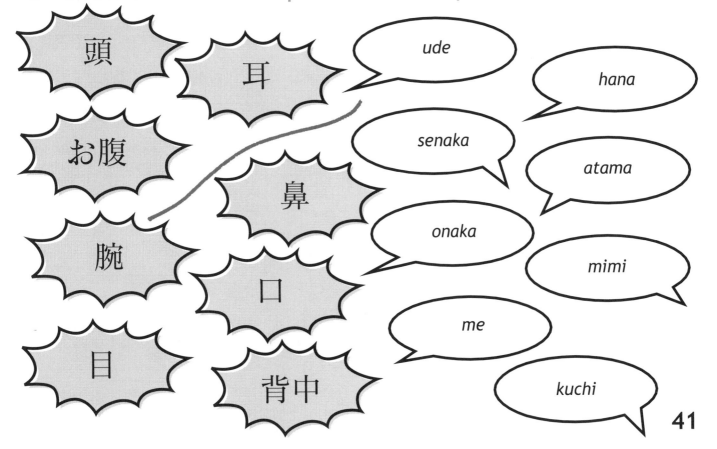

頭

耳

お腹

鼻

腕

口

目

背中

ude

hana

senaka

atama

onaka

mimi

me

kuchi

41

◎ **L**abel the body with the correct number, and write the pronunciation next to the words.

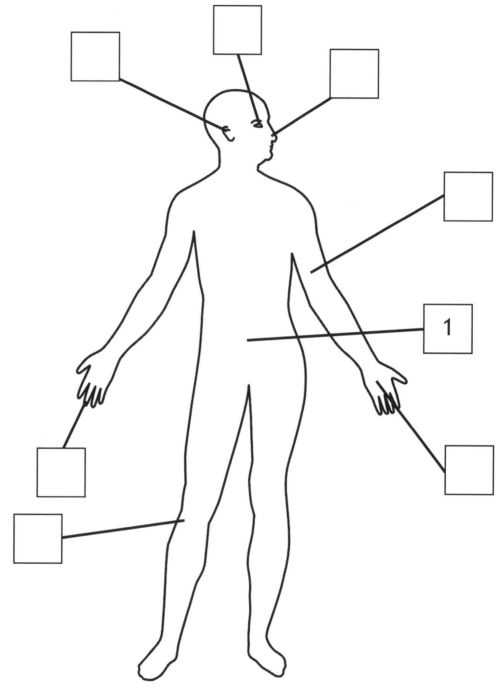

1 お腹 _onaka_   2 腕 _____

3 鼻 _____   4 手 _____

5 耳 _____   6 足 _____

42 7 目 _____   8 指 _____

◎ **F**inally, match the Japanese words, their pronunciation, and the English meanings, as in the example.

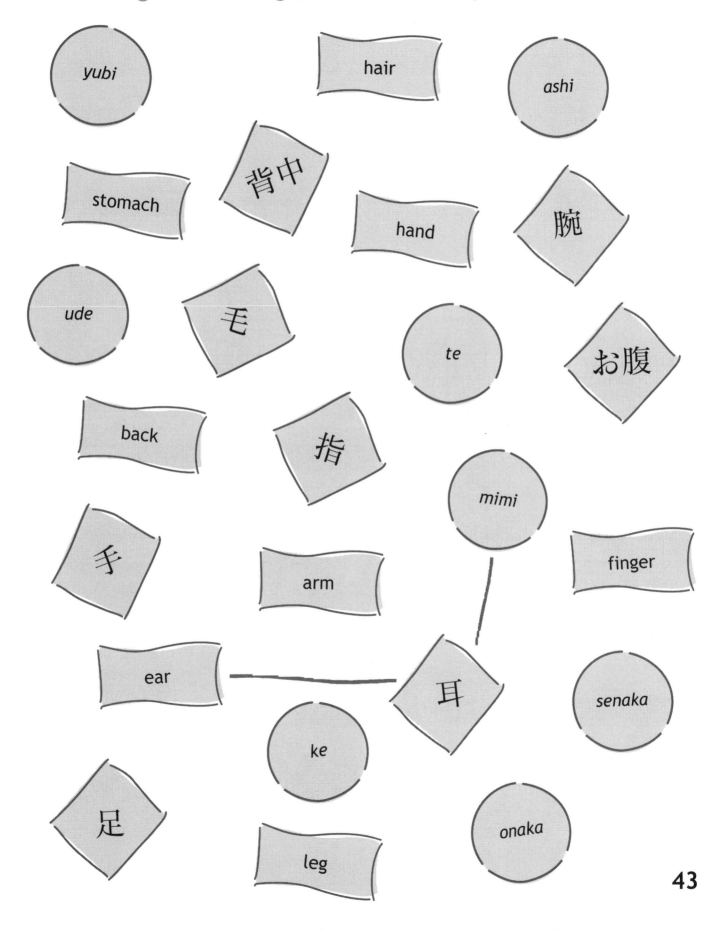

yubi

hair

ashi

stomach

背中

hand

腕

ude

毛

te

お腹

back

指

mimi

finger

手

arm

ear

耳

senaka

ke

足

onaka

leg

8 USEFUL EXPRESSIONS

Look at the pictures.
Tear out the flashcards for this topic.
Follow steps 1 and 2 of the plan in the introduction.

どこ？ *doko*

いいえ
iie

はい
hai

こんにちは
kon'nichiwa

さようなら
sayoonara

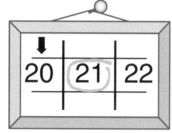

昨日 *kinoo*

今日 *kyoo*

明日 *ash(i)ta*

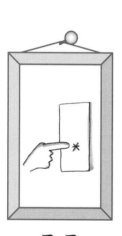

ここ
koko

あそこ *asoko*

今 *ima*

いくら？
ikura

すみません！
sumimasen

すごい！
sugoi

お願い *onegai*

ありがとう
arigatoo

44

Match the Japanese words to their English equivalents.

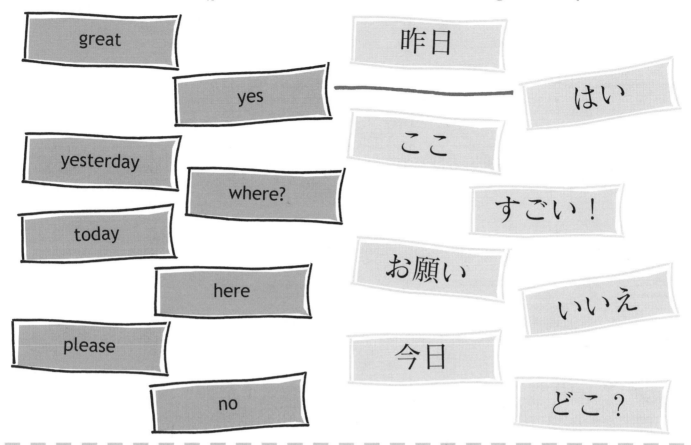

Now match the Japanese to the pronunciation.

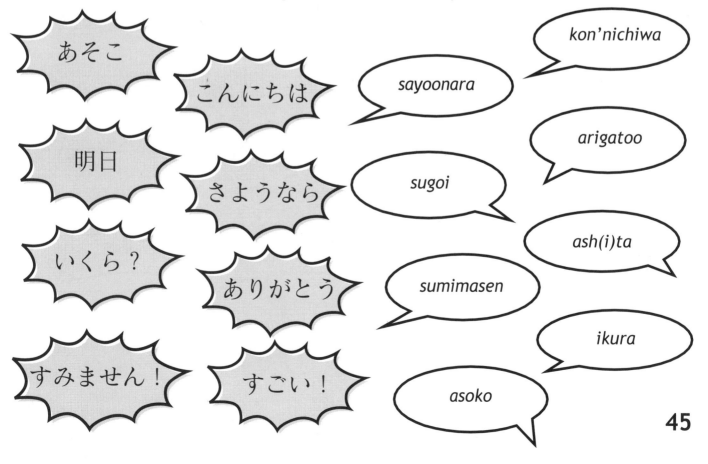

Choose the Japanese word that matches the picture to fill in the English word at the bottom of the page.

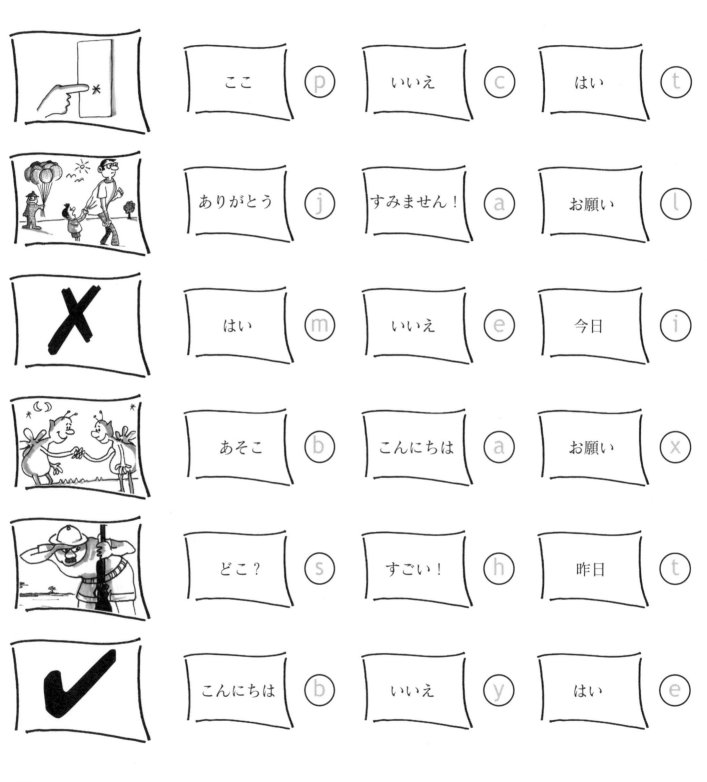

ここ	p	いいえ	c	はい	t
ありがとう	j	すみません！	a	お願い	l
はい	m	いいえ	e	今日	i
あそこ	b	こんにちは	a	お願い	x
どこ？	s	すごい！	h	昨日	t
こんにちは	b	いいえ	y	はい	e

English word: p ○ ○ ○ ○ ○

What are these people saying? Write the correct number in each speech bubble, as in the example.

1. こんにちは 　 2. お願い 　 3. はい 　 4. いいえ

5. ここ 　 6. すみません！ 　 7. どこ？ 　 8. いくら？

Finally, match the Japanese words, their pronunciation, and the English meanings, as in the example.

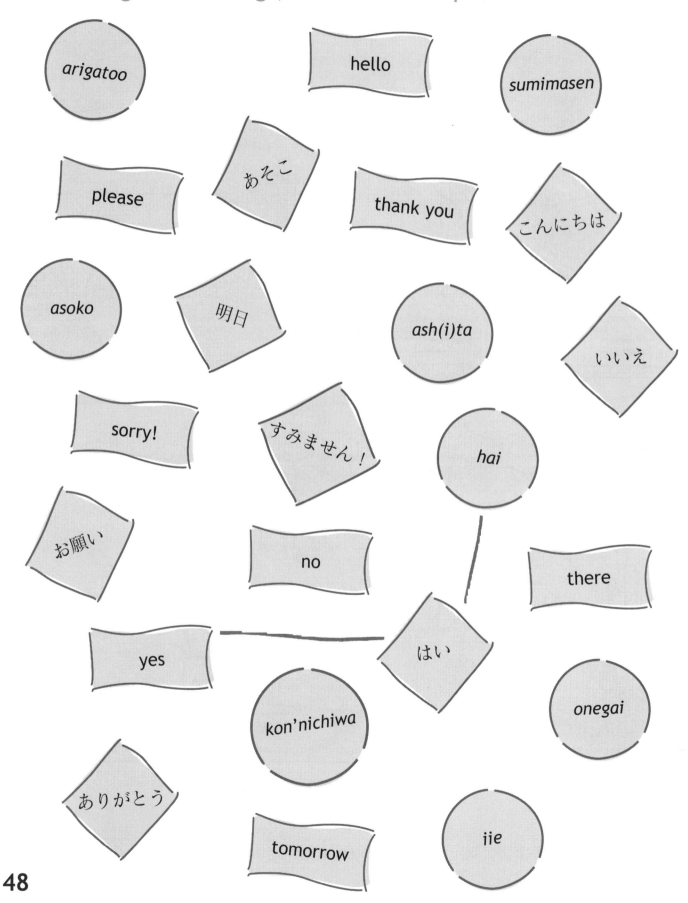

arigatoo

hello

sumimasen

please

あそこ

thank you

こんにちは

asoko

明日

ash(i)ta

いいえ

sorry!

すみません！

hai

お願い

no

there

yes

はい

kon'nichiwa

onegai

ありがとう

tomorrow

iie

● ROUND-UP

This section is designed to review all the 100 words you have met in the different topics. It is a good idea to test yourself with your flashcards before trying this section.

◎ These ten objects are hidden in the picture. Can you find and circle them?

ドア　　　花　　　ベッド　　コート　帽子

自転車　　椅子　　犬　　　魚　　　ソックス

See if you can remember all these words.

今日
バス
速い
鼻
砂漠
はい
戸棚
ライオン
ワンピース
安い
川
足

Find the odd one out in these groups of words and say why.

| 犬 | 牛 | (テーブル) | 猿 |

Because it isn't an animal.

- - - - - - - - -

| 車 | バス | 列車 | 電話 |

- - - - - - - - -

| 畑 | コート | ワイシャツ | スカート |

- - - - - - - - -

| 海 | 湖 | 川 | 木 |

- - - - - - - - -

| 高い | 汚い | きれい | 映画館 |

- - - - - - - - -

| 兎 | 猫 | 魚 | ライオン |

- - - - - - - - -

| 腕 | ソファ | 頭 | お腹 |

- - - - - - - - -

| お願い | 昨日 | 明日 | 今日 |

- - - - - - - - -

| レンジ | ベッド | 戸棚 | 冷蔵庫 |

◎ **L**ook at the objects below for 30 seconds.

◎ **C**over the picture and try to remember all the objects.
Circle the Japanese words for those you remember.

花　　　　　　靴　　　　ありがとう
　　　　　　　　　　　　　　　　　　　　ドア
車　　　　　　　ここ　　　コート　　　列車
　　　いいえ
　　ベルト　　　山　　　　　椅子　　　　馬
　　ソックス　　Tシャツ　　目　　　　ベッド
52　半ズボン　タクシー　　　テレビ　　　猿

Now match the Japanese words, their pronunciation, and the English meanings, as in the example.

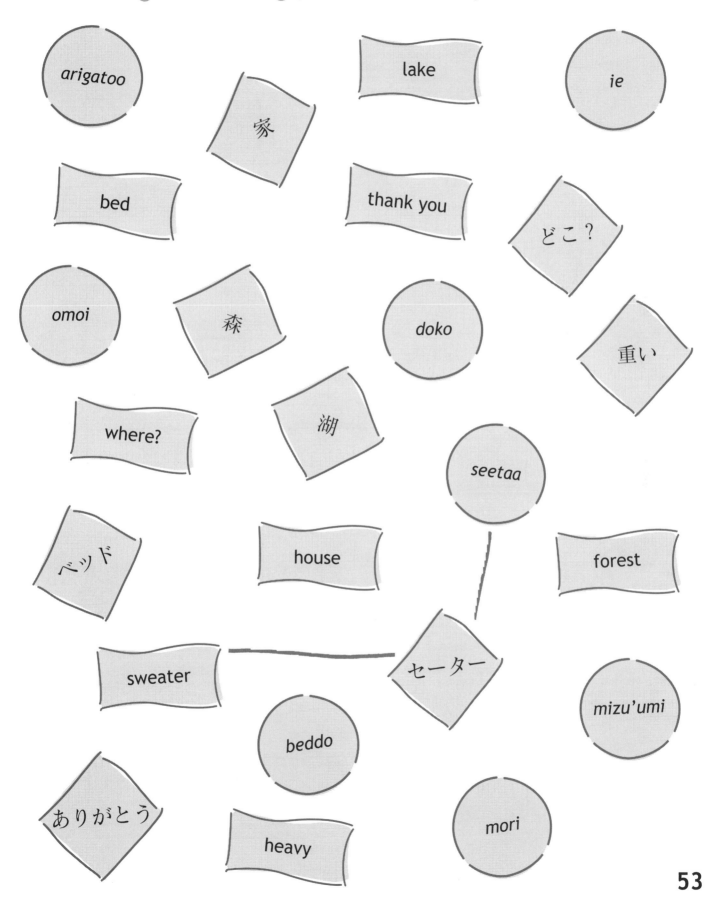

arigatoo

lake

ie

家

bed

thank you

どこ？

omoi

森

doko

重い

where?

湖

seetaa

ベッド

house

forest

sweater

セーター

mizu'umi

beddo

ありがとう

heavy

mori

Fill in the English phrase at the bottom of the page.

Picture	Option 1	Option 2	Option 3
sofa	ソファ (w)	タクシー (g)	耳 (t)
bridge	コート (o)	汚い (a)	橋 (e)
market	はい (m)	いくら？ (l)	今日 (i)
window	牛 (b)	窓 (l)	レストラン (h)
dog	どこ？ (e)	口 (a)	犬 (d)
eye	目 (o)	テーブル (p)	こんにちは (v)
hill	丘 (n)	いいえ (y)	バス (r)
road	兎 (n)	道路 (e)	レンジ (s)

54

English phrase: (w) ◯ ◯ ◯　◯ ◯ ◯ ◯ !

Look at the two pictures and check (✔) the objects that are different in Picture B.

Picture A

Picture B

 半ズボン ☐

 Ｔシャツ ☐

 ドア ☐

 猫 ☐

 椅子 ☐

 魚 ☐

 ソックス ☐

 犬 ☐

Now join the Japanese words to their English equivalents.

refrigerator	腕
pants	お腹
store	小さい
school	冷蔵庫
river	店
great	すごい！
small	川
light	ズボン
arm	きれい
stomach	軽い
clean	馬
horse	学校

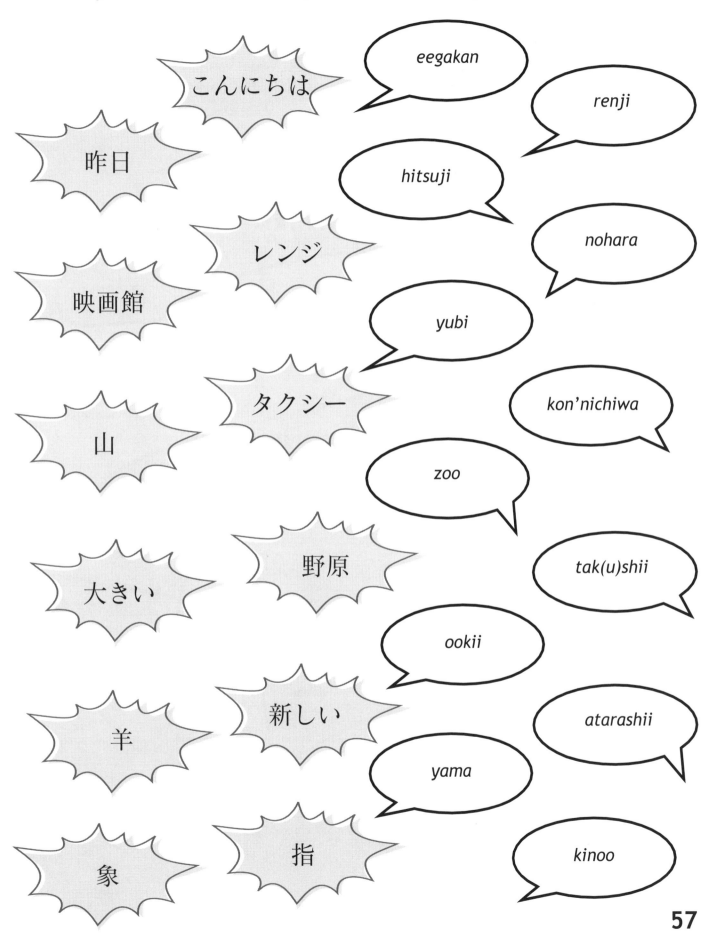

Try to match the Japanese to the pronunciation.

57

Snake game.

- You will need a die and counter(s). You can challenge yourself to reach the finish or play with someone else. You have to throw the exact number to finish.

- Throw the die and move forward that number of spaces. When you land on a word you must pronounce it and say what it means in English. If you can't, you have to go back to the square you came from.

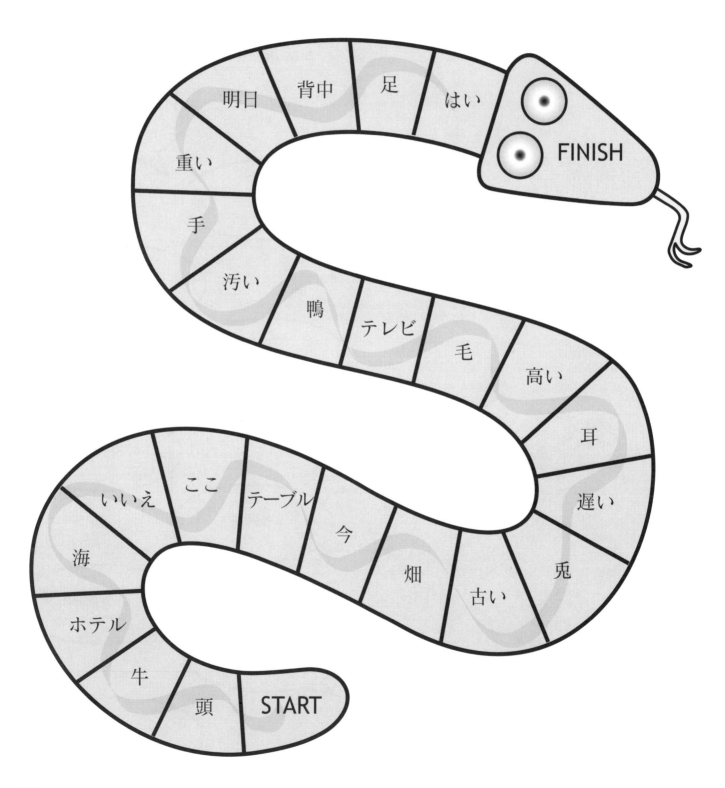

◎ Aɴsᴡᴇʀs

❶ Aʀᴏᴜɴᴅ ᴛʜᴇ ʜᴏᴍᴇ

Page 10 (top)
See page 9 for correct picture.

Page 10 (bottom)

door	ドア
cupboard	戸棚
stove	レンジ
bed	ベッド
table	テーブル
chair	椅子
refrigerator	冷蔵庫
computer	コンピュータ

Page 11 (top)

テーブル	*teeburu*
戸棚	*todana*
コンピュータ	*konpyuutaa*
ベッド	*beddo*
窓	*mado*
電話	*denwa*
テレビ	*terebi*
椅子	*isu*

Page 11 (bottom)

Page 12

Page 13
English word: window

❷ Cʟᴏᴛʜᴇs

Page 15 (top)

ワンピース	*wanpiisu*
半ズボン	*hanzubon*
靴	*kutsu*
ベルト	*beruto*
ワイシャツ	*waishatsu*
Ｔシャツ	*tiishatsu*
帽子	*booshi*
ソックス	*sokk(u)su*

Page 15 (bottom)

Page 16

hat	帽子	*booshi*
shoe	靴	*kutsu*
sock	ソックス	*sokk(u)su*
shorts	半ズボン	*hanzubon*
t-shirt	Ｔシャツ	*tiishatsu*
belt	ベルト	*beruto*
coat	コート	*kooto*
pants	ズボン	*zubon*

Page 17

帽子 (hat)	2
コート (coat)	0
ベルト (belt)	2
靴 (shoe)	2
ズボン (pants)	0
半ズボン (shorts)	2
ワンピース (dress)	1
ソックス (sock)	6 (3 pairs)
スカート (skirt)	1
Ｔシャツ (t-shirt)	3
ワイシャツ(shirt)	0
セーター (sweater)	1

Page 18

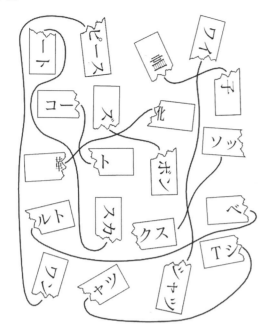

❸ AROUND TOWN

Page 20 (top)

movie theater	映画館
store	店
hotel	ホテル
taxi	タクシー
car	車
train	列車
school	学校
house	家

Page 20 (bottom)

bicycle	4
taxi	7
house	2
bus	1
train	6
road	3
car	5

Page 21

学校

TAXI
タクシー

バス

車

列車

レストラン

ホテル

自転車

Page 22

English word: school

Page 23

バス	*basu*
タクシー	*tak(u)shii*
学校	*gakkoo*
車	*kuruma*
ホテル	*hoteru*
家	*ie*
自転車	*jitensha*
列車	*ressha*
店	*mise*
映画館	*eegakan*
レストラン	*res(u)toran*
道路	*dooro*

❹ COUNTRYSIDE

Page 25

See page 24 for correct picture.

Page 26

橋	✔		野原	✔
木	✔		森	✔
砂漠	✘		湖	✘
丘	✘		川	✔
山	✔		花	✔
海	✘		畑	✔

Page 27 (top)

山	*yama*
川	*kawa*
森	*mori*
砂漠	*sabaku*
海	*umi*
畑	*hatake*
橋	*hashi*
野原	*nohara*

湖	べ	き	車	き	ド	中	コ
ト	タ	ン	ピ	映	ト	丘	ン
ス	汚	畑	棚	ス	い	耳	帽
速	い	す	よ	な	い	に	ン
子	い	イ	足	花	く	鼠	校
お	兎	い	新	い	口	路	ス
木	蔵	兎	ラ	ン	一	橋	ン
ト	店	ボ	羊	ツ	み	す	ん

Page 28

sea	海	*umi*
lake	湖	*mizu'umi*
desert	砂漠	*sabaku*
farm	畑	*hatake*
flower	花	*hana*
mountain	山	*yama*
river	川	*kawa*
field	野原	*nohara*

❺ OPPOSITES

Page 30

expensive	高い
big	大きい
light	軽い
slow	遅い
clean	きれい
inexpensive	安い
dirty	汚い
small	小さい
heavy	重い
new	新しい
fast	速い
old	古い

Page 31

English word: change

Page 32

Odd one outs are those which are not opposites:
重い
小さい
新しい
汚い
遅い
安い

Page 33

old	新しい
big	小さい
new	古い
slow	速い
dirty	きれい
small	大きい
heavy	軽い
clean	汚い
light	重い
expensive	安い
inexpensive	高い

❻ ANIMALS

Page 35

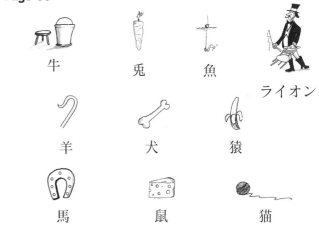

牛　　兎　　魚　　ライオン

羊　　犬　　猿

馬　　鼠　　猫

Page 36

兎	*usagi*
馬	*uma*
猿	*saru*
犬	*inu*
猫	*neko*
鼠	*nezumi*
鴨	*kamo*
魚	*sakana*
ライオン	*raion*
羊	*hitsuji*
牛	*ushi*
象	*zoo*

Page 37

elephant	✔	mouse	✘
monkey	✘	cat	✔
sheep	✔	dog	✘
lion	✔	cow	✔
fish	✔	horse	✘
duck	✘	rabbit	✔

Page 38

monkey	猿
cow	牛
mouse	鼠
dog	犬
sheep	羊
fish	魚
lion	ライオン
elephant	象
cat	猫
duck	鴨
rabbit	兎
horse	馬

❼ PARTS OF THE BODY

Page 40

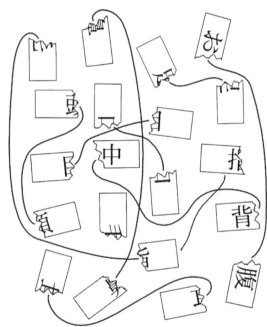

Page 41 (top)

You should have also drawn pictures of:

leg; mouth; ear; nose; eye; hair

Page 41 (bottom)

頭	*atama*
耳	*mimi*
お腹	*onaka*
鼻	*hana*
腕	*ude*
口	*kuchi*
目	*me*
背中	*senaka*

Page 42

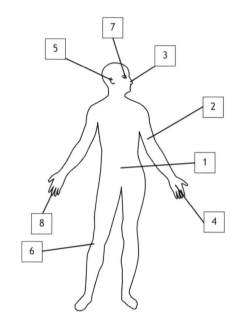

1.	お腹	*onaka*
2.	腕	*ude*
3.	鼻	*hana*
4.	手	*te*
5.	耳	*mimi*
6.	足	*ashi*
7.	目	*me*
8.	指	*yubi*

Page 43

ear	耳	*mimi*
hair	毛	*ke*
hand	手	*te*
stomach	お腹	*onaka*
arm	腕	*ude*
back	背中	*senaka*
finger	指	*yubi*
leg	足	*ashi*

8 USEFUL EXPRESSIONS

Page 45 (top)

great	すごい！
yes	はい
yesterday	昨日
where?	どこ？
today	今日
here	ここ
please	お願い
no	いいえ

Page 45 (bottom)

あそこ	*asoko*
こんにちは	*kon'nichiwa*
明日	*ash(i)ta*
さようなら	*sayoonara*
いくら？	*ikura*
ありがとう	*arigatoo*
すみません！	*sumimasen*
すごい！	*sugoi*

Page 46

English word: please

Page 47

Page 48

yes	はい	*hai*
hello	こんにちは	*kon'nichiwa*
no	いいえ	*iie*
sorry	すみません！	*sumimasen*
please	お願い	*onegai*
there	あそこ	*asoko*
thank you	ありがとう	*arigatoo*
tomorrow	明日	*ash(i)ta*

● ROUND-UP

Page 49

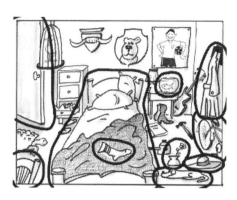

Page 50

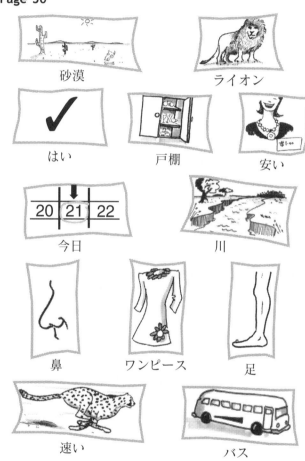

砂漠　　ライオン

はい　　戸棚　　安い

今日　　川

鼻　　ワンピース　　足

速い　　バス

Page 51

テーブル (Because it isn't an animal.)

電話 (Because it isn't a means of transportation.)

畑 (Because it isn't an item of clothing.)

木 (Because it isn't connected with water.)

映画館 (Because it isn't a descriptive word.)

魚 (Because it lives in water/doesn't have legs.)

ソファ (Because it isn't a part of the body.)

お願い (Because it isn't an expression of time.)

ベッド (Because you wouldn't find it in the kitchen.)

Page 52

Words that appear in the picture:
Ｔシャツ
車
花
靴
列車
猿
テレビ
椅子
ベルト
半ズボン

Page 53

sweater	セーター	seetaa
lake	湖	mizu'umi
thank you	ありがとう	arigatoo
bed	ベッド	beddo
house	家	ie
forest	森	mori
where?	どこ？	doko
heavy	重い	omoi

Page 54

English phrase: well done!

Page 55

半ズボン	✔ (shade)
Ｔシャツ	✘
ドア	✔ (handle)
猫	✘
椅子	✔ (back)
魚	✔ (direction)
ソックス	✔ (pattern)
犬	✘

Page 56

refrigerator	冷蔵庫
pants	ズボン
store	店
school	学校
river	川
great	すごい！
small	小さい
light	軽い
arm	腕
stomach	お腹
clean	きれい
horse	馬

Page 57

こんにちは	kon'nichiwa
昨日	kinoo
レンジ	renji
映画館	eegakan
タクシー	tak(u)shii
山	yama
野原	nohara
大きい	ookii
新しい	atarashii
羊	hitsuji
指	yubi
象	zoo

Page 58

Here are the English equivalents of the word, in order from START to FINISH:

(For the pronunciation, see the relevant topic page.)

head *atama*	farm *hatake*	duck *kamo*
cow *ushi*	old *furui*	dirty *kitanai*
hotel *hoteru*	rabbit *usagi*	hand *te*
sea *umi*	slow *osoi*	heavy *omoi*
no *iie*	ear *mimi*	tomorrow *ash(i)ta*
here *koko*	expensive *takai*	back *senaka*
table *teeburu*	hair *ke*	leg *ashi*
now *ima*	television *terebi*	yes *hai*

ベルト
beruto

コート
kooto

スカート
s(u)kaato

帽子
booshi

Ｔシャツ
tiishatsu

靴
kutsu

セーター
seetaa

ワイシャツ
waishatsu

半ズボン
hanzubon

ソックス
sokk(u)su

ズボン
zubon

ワンピース
wanpiisu

coat	belt
hat	skirt
shoe	t-shirt
shirt	sweater
sock	shorts
dress	pants

学校 *gakkoo*	車 *kuruma*
道路 *dooro*	映画館 *eegakan*
ホテル *hoteru*	店 *mise*
タクシー *tak(u)shii*	自転車 *jitensha*
レストラン *res(u)toran*	バス *basu*
列車 *ressha*	家 *ie*

car	school
movie theater	road
store	hotel
bicycle	taxi
bus	restaurant
house	train

湖
mizu'umi

森
mori

丘
oka

海
umi

山
yama

木
ki

砂漠
sabaku

花
hana

橋
hashi

川
kawa

畑
hatake

野原
nohara

forest	lake
sea	hill
tree	mountain
flower	desert
river	bridge
field	farm

重い
omoi

軽い
karui

大きい
ookii

小さい
chiisai

古い
furui

新しい
atarashii

速い
hayai

遅い
osoi

きれい
kiree

汚い
kitanai

安い
yasui

高い
takai

light	heavy
small	big
new	old
slow	fast
dirty	clean
expensive	cheap

鴨
kamo

猫
neko

鼠
nezumi

牛
ushi

兎
usagi

犬
inu

馬
uma

猿
saru

ライオン
raion

魚
sakana

象
zoo

羊
hitsuji

❻ ANIMALS

cat	duck
cow	mouse
dog	rabbit
monkey	horse
fish	lion
sheep	elephant

腕
ude

指
yubi

頭
atama

口
kuchi

耳
mimi

足
ashi

手
te

お腹
onaka

目
me

毛
ke

鼻
hana

背中
senaka

finger	arm
mouth	head
leg	ear
stomach	hand
hair	eye
back	nose

お願い
onegai

ありがとう
arigatoo

はい
hai

いいえ
iie

こんにちは
kon'nichiwa

さようなら
sayoonara

昨日
kinoo

今日
kyoo

明日
ash(i)ta

どこ？
doko

ここ
koko

あそこ
asoko

すみません！
sumimasen

いくら？
ikura

すごい！
sugoi

今
ima

thank you	please
no	yes
goodbye	hello
today	yesterday
where?	tomorrow
there	here
how much?	sorry!
now	great!